D0572595

First Facts®

ANCIENT EGYPT

PYRAMIDS

BY KREMENA SPENGLER

Consultant:
Leo Depuydt
Professor, Department of Egyptology
and Ancient Western Asian Studies
Brown University,
Providence, Rhode Island

Capstone
press®

Mankato, Minnesota

First Facts are published by Capstone Press,
151 Good Counsel Drive, P.O. Box 669, Mankato, Minnesota 56002.
www.capstonepress.com

Library of Congress Cataloging-in-Publication Data
Spengler, Kremena.
    Pyramids / by Kremena Spengler.
    p. cm. — (First facts. Ancient Egypt)
    Summary: "Describes the pyramids of ancient Egypt, including how and why they were
built" — Provided by publisher.
    Includes bibliographical references and index.
    ISBN-13: 978-1-4296-1915-8 (hardcover)
    ISBN-10: 1-4296-1915-5 (hardcover) 3970 9901 2/09
    1. Pyramids — Egypt — Juvenile literature. I. Title. II. Series.
DT63.S64 2009
932 — dc22   2007050519

Editorial Credits
Jennifer Besel, editor; Alison Thiele, designer; Wanda Winch, photo researcher;
    Marcy Morin, page 21 project production

Photo Credits
AP Images/Amr Nabil, 8–9; AP Images/Mohammad al sehety, 13 (right); The Art Archive/Gianni Dagli Orti, 11
(right); Art Resource, N.Y./ Werner Forman, 12–13; The Bridgeman Art Library International/Private
Collection/Where Egypt's Kings of old were buried, illustration from 'Newnes' Pictorial Book of Knowledge'
(colour litho), Tennant, Dudley C. (fl.1898-1918), 10–11; Capstone Press/Karon Dubke, 21; Getty Images Inc./
Stone/Will & Deni McIntyre, 17; Shutterstock/Andre Klaassen, cover; Shutterstock/Ian Stewart, 18–19;
Shutterstock/Mikhail Nekrasov, 20; Shutterstock/Pichugin Dmitry, 4–5, 16; Shutterstock/Salem Alforaih, 1;
Shutterstock/Svetlana Privezentseva, 6–7; Shutterstock/Vladimir Korostyshevskiy, 14–15; Shutterstock/YKh,
background throughout

Essential content terms are bold and are defined at the bottom of the page where they first appear.

TABLE OF CONTENTS

Amazing Builders

Imagine putting together a 480-foot-tall (146-meter-tall) pyramid. And each block weighs as much as 25 refrigerators. About 4,500 years ago, the Egyptians did just that. They didn't have trucks or cranes to help them, either. They used ramps and strength to put the blocks in place.

Ancient Egypt

The time in history called ancient Egypt began around 3000 BC, about 5,000 years ago. It ended in 30 BC, when Rome took over Egypt.

5

A TOMB FOR A KING

In Egypt, **pharaohs** were believed to be like gods. Egyptians believed the kings needed their bodies after death. That meant the bodies needed safe resting places. The pyramids were built to be **tombs** for Egypt's kings.

pharaoh: a king in ancient Egypt

tomb: a room for holding a dead body

Egypt's first pyramid,
the step pyramid of Djoser

WHERE ARE THE PYRAMIDS?

The Egyptians built the pyramids west of the Nile River. They believed the dead entered life after death through the west.

The pyramids were built in the desert. The soil along the Nile was good for growing food. The pyramids were not built in this important area.

HOW THEY DID IT

Building the pyramids took years. Workers used hand tools to cut blocks in a **quarry**. Then they dragged the blocks on sleds to the building sites. They floated other blocks on boats along the Nile River. Builders used ramps to move the blocks into place.

quarry: a place where stone is dug from the ground

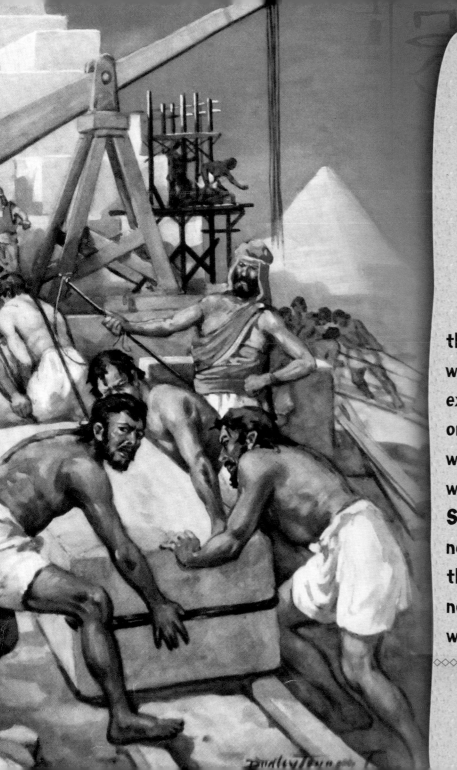

PYRAMID BUILDERS

Archaeologists once thought the pyramid builders were slaves. But as they explored, they found writing on the pyramid walls. The writing showed the builders were proud of their work. Scientists also found villages nearby with hospitals to treat the builders. Today, scientists no longer believe the builders were slaves.

archaeologist: a person who studies the past by digging up old objects

INSIDE THE PYRAMIDS

Pyramids have many tunnels and rooms. Each pyramid has a hidden room called the burial **chamber**. The pharaoh's coffin was placed there.

Scribes often carved prayers into the walls. These words would help the king after death.

chamber: a large room

scribe: a person in ancient Egypt who wrote for other people

prayers carved in the pyramid of Unas

ROBOTS IN PYRAMIDS

Scientists use robots with cameras to explore inside pyramids. One robot showed scientists a new door inside the Great Pyramid. In the future, robots might be able to show other things hidden deep inside.

entrance to the Great Pyramid blocked by heavy stones

HIDDEN TREASURES

Ancient Egyptians believed pharaohs needed treasures after death. They placed furniture, food, and gold in the pyramids.

To stop thieves, builders blocked doorways with stones. Some thieves still dug their way in. They stole most of the treasures.

THE PYRAMIDS OF GIZA

The greatest pyramids are at a place called Giza. The Great Pyramid is the largest ever built. It is made of about 2 million stone blocks.

Great Pyramid

King Khafre's pyramid

The second largest pyramid at Giza was built for King Khafre. Visitors can see the **temples** that were built around this pyramid.

temple: a building used for worship

DISCOVER!

Each block in the Great Pyramid weighs more than 2 tons (1.8 metric tons).

The smallest Giza pyramid was for King Menkaure. But it's not that small. This pyramid is 203 feet (62 meters) tall.

Long ago, the pyramids were built to honor kings. But today, the pyramids teach us about life in ancient Egypt.

DISCOVER!

More than 20,000 workers built the pyramids at Giza. It took the workers at least 80 years to finish them.

The Great Sphinx was cut out of rock near Khafre's pyramid. No one knows why the Sphinx was built. Whatever its purpose, the Sphinx is an amazing statue. It stands 66 feet (20 meters) high. And the Sphinx is 187 feet (57 meters) long.

HANDS ON: SUGARY PYRAMID

The ancient Egyptians built pyramids from heavy rock. You probably can't do that, but you can build a pyramid from sugar cubes.

What You Need

- ✦ pastry brush
- ✦ white icing
- ✦ 91 sugar cubes

What You Do

1. Use the brush and icing to glue together six rows of six sugar cubes each. Glue the rows into a square base.

2. For the second layer, glue together five rows of five cubes each. Center and glue this layer on top of the base.

3. Repeat four more times. Each time, decrease the rows by one cube. The top row will be a single cube.

GLOSSARY

archaeologist (ar-kee-OL-uh-jist) — a person who learns about the past by digging up old buildings or objects and studying them

chamber (CHAYM-bur) — a large room

pharaoh (FAIR-oh) — a king of ancient Egypt

quarry (KWOR-ee) — a place where stone is dug from the ground

scribe (SKRIBE) — a writer in ancient Egypt trained to read and write hieroglyphs

temple (TEM-puhl) — a building used for worship

tomb (TOOM) — a grave, room, or building used to hold a dead body

READ MORE

Filer, Joyce. *Pyramids*. New York: Oxford University Press, 2005.

Leardi, Jeanette. *The Great Pyramid: Egypt's Tomb for All Time*. Castles, Palaces & Tombs. New York: Bearport, 2007.

Williams, Brenda, and Brian Williams. *Reach for the Stars: Ancient Egyptian Pyramids*. Fusion. Chicago: Raintree, 2008.

INTERNET SITES

FactHound offers a safe, fun way to find Internet sites related to this book. All of the sites on FactHound have been researched by our staff.

Here's how:
1. Visit *www.facthound.com*
2. Choose your grade level.
3. Type in this book ID **1429619155** for age-appropriate sites. You may also browse subjects by clicking on letters, or by clicking on pictures and words.
4. Click on the **Fetch It** button.

FactHound will fetch the best sites for you!

INDEX